T0193401

# Words

## for the Soul

Language Unlimited

Scroll 1

R W  M A R T N

authorHOUSE®

AuthorHouse™
1663 Liberty Drive
Bloomington, IN 47403
www.authorhouse.com
Phone: 833-262-8899

Published by AuthorHouse 07/29/2023

ISBN: 979-8-8230-1150-1 (sc)
ISBN: 979-8-8230-1231-7 (hc)
ISBN: 979-8-8230-1153-2 (e)

Library of Congress Control Number: 2023913689

Print information available on the last page.

This book is printed on acid-free paper.

# THE LORD'S PRAYER:
## (Language Unlimited)

*This scroll is the beginning of a series of relational prayer where language knows no bounds.*

Scripture
**Matthew 6:9-13**

6:9
After this manner therefore pray ye: Our Father which art in heaven, Hallowed be thy name.

6:10
Thy kingdom come. Thy will be done in earth, as it is in heaven.

6:11
Give us this day our daily bread.

6:12
And forgive us our debts, as we forgive our debtors.

6:13
And lead us not into temptation, but deliver us from evil: For thine is the kingdom, and the power, and the glory, for ever. Amen.

**SOURCE:**
*Holy Bible*
*American Bible Society, 2011*
King James Version
KJV 400th Anniversary
ISBN: 978-1-58516-986-3

# CONTENTS

# AFRIKAANS

Skrif
Matteus 6:9–13

6:9
Daarom bid julle dan: Ons Vader wat in die hemel is, laat u Naam geheilig word.

6:10
Laat u koninkryk kom. Laat u wil op die aarde geskied, soos in die hemel.

6:11
Gee ons vandag ons daaglikse brood.

6:12
En vergeef ons ons skulde, soos ons ons skuldenaars vergewe.

6:13
En lei ons nie in versoeking nie, maar verlos ons van die bose: Want U is die koninkryk en die krag en die heerlikheid tot in ewigheid. Amen.

# ALBANIAN

Shkrimi
Mateu 6:9–13

6:9
Lutjuni, pra, kështu: Ati ynë që je në qiej, u shenjtëroftë emri yt.

6:10
Ardhtë mbretëria jote. U bëftë vullneti yt në tokë, ashtu si në qiell.

6:11
Na jep sot bukën tonë të përditshme.

6:12
Dhe na fal borxhet tona, ashtu siç i falim ne debitorët tanë.

6:13
Dhe mos na ço në tundim, por na çliro nga i ligu, sepse jotja është mbretëria, fuqia dhe lavdia përjetë. Amin.

# AMHARIC

ቅዱሳት መጻሕፍት
ማቴዎስ 6:9–13


6:9
ስለዚህ እንዲህ ጸልዩ፦ በሰማያት የምትኖር አባታችን ሆይ፣ ስምህ ይቀደስ።

6:10
መንግሥትህ ትምጣ። ፈቃድህ በሰማይ እንደ ሆነች እንዲሁ በምድር ትሁን።

6:11–13
የዕለት እንጀራችንን ዛሬ ስጠን። ከክፉ አድነን እንጂ ወደ ፈተና አታግባን፤
መንግሥት ያንተ ናትና ኃይልም ክብርም ለዘለዓለሙ። አሜን

# ARABIC

الكتاب المقدس
متى 9-13 :6

6:9
بعد هذا اذه صلوا :أبا انا الذي في السماوات ، ليتقدس اسمك.

6:10
ليأت ملكوتك. لتكن مشيئتك كما في السماء في الأرض كما في السماء.

6:11
أعطنا انا اذه خبزز انا اليومي.

6:12
واغفر لنا ديوننا ، كما نغفر نحن ايضا مدينينا.

6:13
ولا تدخلنا في تجربة لب نجنا من الشرير لأن لك الملكوت والقوة والمجد إلى الأبد. آمين.

4

# ARMENIAN

Սուրբ Գիրք Մատթեոս 6:9–13


6:9
Ուրեմն այսպես աղոթեք. Հայր մեր, որ երկնքում ես, սուրբ լինի քո անունը:

6:10
գա քո թագավորությունը: Քո կամքը թող լինի երկրի վրա, ինչպես որ երկնքում է:

6:11
Տուր մեզ այսօր մեր ամենօրյա հացը:

6:12
Եվ ներիր մեզ մեր պարտքերը, ինչպես մենք ենք ներում մեր պարտապաններին:

6:13
Եվ մի՛ տանիր մեզ փորձության մեջ, այլ փրկիր մեզ չարից, որովհետև քոնն է թագավորությունը և զորությունը և փառքը հավիտյան: Ամեն.

# AYMARA

Qullan Qillqatanaka
Mateo 6:9–13

6:9
Ukhamasti akham mayisipxam: Alaxpachankir Awkixa, sutimax
jach'añchatäpan —sasa.

6:10
Juman reinomax jutpan. Munañamax aka uraqin luratäpan,
kunjämtix alaxpachan luraski ukhama.

6:11
Jichhürojj sapa uru t'ant'a churapjjeta.

6:12
Ukat juchanakas pampachapxita, kunjamtï jiwasax manükistu
ukanakar pampachktan ukhama.

6:13
Jan yant'äwir irpapxita, jan ukasti ñanqhat qhispiyapxita, juman
reinopasa, ch'amapasa, jach'a kankañapasa wiñayataki. Amén.

# AZERBAIJANI

Müqəddəs Yazılar
Matta 6:9–13

6:9
Bu əkildə dua edin: Göylərdə olan Atamız, adın müqəddəs tutulsun.

6:10
Sənin Pad ahlı ın gəlsin. Göydə oldu u kimi yerdə də Sənin iradən yerinə yetsin.

6:11
Bu gün bizə gündəlik çörəyimizi ver.

6:12
Və borclarımızı ba ı ladı ımız kimi, bizim də borclarımızı ba ı la.

6:13
Bizi sına a çəkmə, bizi ərdən xilas et: Çünki pad ahlıq, qüdrət və izzət əbədi olaraq sənindir. Amin.

# BELARUSIAN

Святое Пісанне
Мацвея 6:9–13

6:9
Маліцеся такім чынам: Ойча наш, Які ёсць на нябёсах, хай свяціцца імя Тваё.

6:10
Прыйдзі Валадарства Тваё. Хай будзе воля Твая як на небе, так і на зямлі.

6:11
Хлеба нашага надзённага дай нам сёння.

6:12
І даруй нам правіны нашы, як і мы даруем вінаватым нашым.

6:13
І не ўвядзі нас у спакусу, але збаў нас ад злога, бо Тваё ёсць Царства, і сіла, і слава навекі. Амін.

# BENGALI

ধর্মগ্রন্থ
ম্যাথু 6:9–13

6:9
এই পদ্ধতির পরে তোমরা প্রার্থনা কর: আমাদের স্বর্গের
পিতা, তোমার নাম পবিত্র হোক।

6:10
তোমার রাজ্য আসুক তোমার ইচ্ছা যেমন স্বর্গে তেমনি
পৃথিবীতেও পূর্ণ হয়।

6:11–13
আজকে আমাদের প্রতিদিনের রুটি দাও।
এবং আমাদের প্রলোভনের মধ্যে নিয়ে যাবেন না, কিন্তু
আমাদের মন্দ থেকে উদ্ধার করুন: আপনার রাজ্য, শক্তি এবং
গৌরব চিরকালের জন্য। আমীন।

# BHOJPURI

शास्त्र के बारे में बतावल गइल बा
मत्ती 6:9–13 में दिहल गइल बा

6:9
एही से तू लोग एही तरह से प्रार्थना करीं कि हमनी के पिता जे स्वर्ग में बानी, तोहार नाम पवित्र होखे।

6:10
तोहार राज आ जा। तोहार इच्छा धरती पर भी होखे, जइसे स्वर्ग में होला।

6:11
आज हमनी के रोज के रोटी दे दऽ।

6:12
आ हमनी के कर्जा माफ करऽ, जइसे हमनी के अपना कर्जा के माफ कर देनी जा।

6:13
आ हमनी के परीक्षा में मत डालीं, बलुक बुराई से बचाईं; काहे कि राज्य, शक्ति आ महिमा हमेशा खातिर तोहार हा। आमीन के कहल जाला।

# BOSNIAN

Sveto pismo
Matej 6:9–13

6:9
Na ovaj na in se molite: O e naš koji jesi na nebesima, da se sveti ime tvoje.

6:10
Da do e kraljevstvo tvoje. Neka bude volja Tvoja i na zemlji, kao i na nebu.

6:11
Hljeb naš nasušni daj nam danas.

6:12
I oprosti nam dugove naše, kao što i mi opraštamo dužnicima našim.

6:13
I ne uvedi nas u iskušenje, nego nas izbavi od zla: jer je tvoje kraljevstvo i sila i slava dovijeka. Amen.

# BULGARIAN

Писание
Матей 6:9–13

6:9
Молете се вие по следния начин: Отче наш, Който си на небесата, да се свети Твоето име.

6:10
Да дойде Твоето царство. Да бъде Твоята воля, както на небето, така и на земята.

6:11
Насъщния ни хляб дай ни днес.

6:12
И прости ни дълговете, както и ние прощаваме на нашите длъжници.

6:13
И не ни въвеждай в изкушение, но избави ни от лукавия: защото Твое е царството, и силата, и славата до века. Амин.

# BURMESE

ကျမ်းဂန်
မဿဲ ၆:၉-၁၃

၆:၉
ဗိုတ်ျ ကောင်း ကင်ဘုံ၌ ရှိတော်မူသော ငါတို့အဘ၊ ကိုယ်တော်၏နာမတော်အား ရိုသေခြင်းရှိပါစေသော။

၆:၁၀
မင်းကြီး လာမယ်။ အလိုတော်သည် ကောင်းကင်ဘုံ၌ ရှိသကဲ့သို့ မြေကြီး၌ ပြည့်စုံပါစေသော။

၆:၁၁
ယနေ့ကျွေးမွေးတော်မူ၍နေ့စဉ်မပြတ်ပေးပါ။

၆:၁၂
ကြွေးများကို လွှတ်သကဲ့သို့ ငါတို့အကြွေးများကို လွှတ်ကပြလော့။

၆:၁၃
စုံးနှောင့်ရှုက်ခြင်းသို့ မလိုက်ဆောင်ဘဲ၊ ဘေးဥပဒ်မှ ကယ်နှုတ်တော်မူပါ။ အာမင်။

# CATALAN

Escriptura
Mateu 6:9–13

6:9
Pregueu, doncs, d'aquesta manera: Pare nostre que ets al cel, santificat sigui el teu nom.

6:10
Venga el teu regne. Es faci la teva voluntat a la terra, com al cel.

6:11
Dóna'ns avui el nostre pa de cada dia.

6:12
I perdona'ns els nostres deutes, com nosaltres perdonem als nostres deutors.

6:13
I no ens deixis a la temptació, sinó allibera'ns del mal: perquè teu és el regne, el poder i la glòria per sempre. Amén.

# CEBUANO

Kasulatan
Mateo 6:9–13

6:9
Busa pag-ampo kamo sa ingon niini nga paagi: Amahan namo nga anaa sa langit, pagabalaanon unta ang imong ngalan.

6:10
Umanhi ang imong gingharian. Matuman ang imong pagbuot dinhi sa yuta, maingon sa langit.

6:11
Ihatag kanamo karong adlawa ang among kalan-on sa matag-adlaw.

6:12
Ug pasayloa kami sa among mga utang, ingon nga nagapasaylo kami sa mga nakautang kanamo.

6:13
Ug ayaw kami itugyan sa panulay, kondili luwasa kami gikan sa dautan: Kay imo ang gingharian, ug ang gahum, ug ang himaya, hangtud sa kahangturan. Amen.

# CHICHEWA

Malemba
Mateyu 6:9–13

6:9
Chifukwa chake pempherani inu chomwechi: Atate wathu wa Kumwamba, Dzina lanu liyeretsedwe.

6:10
Ufumu wanu udze. Kufuna kwanu kuchitidwe, monga Kumwamba chomwecho pansi pano.

6:11
Mutipatse ife lero chakudya chathu chatsiku ndi tsiku.

6:12
Ndipo mutikhululukire mangawa athu, monga ifenso tikhululukira amangawa athu.

6:13
Ndipo musatitengere ife kokatiyesa, koma mutipulumutse ife kwa woyipayo: Pakuti wanu uli ufumu, ndi mphamvu, ndi ulemerero, kwanthawizonse. Amene.

# CHINESE SIMPLIFIED

圣经
马太福音 6:9–13

6:9
因此，你们要这样祷告：我们在天上的父，愿人都尊你的名为圣。

6:10
愿你的国降临。 你的旨意行在地上，如同行在天上。

6:11
给我们这一天我们日用的饮食。

6:12
并免除我们的债务，就像我们免除债务人一样。

6:13
不叫我们遇见试探，救我们脱离凶恶：因为国度、权柄、荣耀，都是你的，直到永远。 阿门。

# CHINESE TRADITIONAL

聖經
馬太福音 6:9–13

6:9
因此，你們要這樣禱告：我們在天上的父，願人都尊你的名為聖。

6:10
願你的國降臨。 你的旨意行在地上，如同行在天上。

6:11
給我們這一天我們日用的飲食。

6:12
並免除我們的債務，就像我們免除債務人一樣。

6:13
不叫我們遇見試探，救我們脫離兇惡：因為國度、權柄、榮耀，都是你的，直到永遠。 阿門。

# CROATIAN

Sveto pismo
Matej 6:9–13

6:9
Molite se dakle ovako: O e naš koji jesi na nebesima, sveti se ime tvoje.

6:10
Do i kraljevstvo tvoje. Neka bude volja tvoja kako na nebu tako i na zemlji.

6:11
Hljeb naš svagdašnji daj nam danas.

6:12
I oprosti nam duge naše kako i mi otpuštamo dužnicima svojim.

6:13
I ne uvedi nas u napast, nego nas izbavi od zla: Jer tvoje je kraljevstvo i mo i slava u vijeke vjekova. Amen.

# CZECH

Posvátná kniha
Matouš 6:9–13

6:9
Po tomto zp sobu se tedy modlete: Ot e náš, jenž jsi na nebesích, posv se jméno tvé.

6:10
P ij království tvé. Bu v le tvá jako v nebi, tak i na zemi.

6:11
Chléb náš vezdejší dej nám dnes.

6:12
A odpus nám naše dluhy, jako my odpouštíme našim dlužník m.

6:13
A neuve nás v pokušení, ale vysvobo nás od zlého, nebo tvé je království a moc a sláva na v ky. Amen.

# DANISH

Skriften
Matthæus 6:9–13

6:9
Bed derfor på denne måde: Vor Fader, som er i himlene,
helliget være dit navn.

6:10
Komme dit rige. Din vilje ske på jorden, som den sker i himlen.

6:11
Giv os i dag vort daglige brød.

6:12
Og eftergiv os vores gæld, som vi tilgiver vores skyldnere.

6:13
Og led os ikke ind i fristelse, men fri os fra det onde: For dit er
riget og magten og æren for evigt. Amen.

# DHIVEHI

ދުޢާ ކުރުމާއި ރޯދަ

މަތީ 6:9-13 ހަމައަށް

**6:9**

ތިޔަބައިމީހުން ދުޢާ ކުރާނީ މިފަދައިންނެވެ.

**6:10**

އަޅަމެންގެ ވެރި ރަސްކަލާނގެ ރަސްކަންފުޅު އަންނާށިއެވެ. ކަލޭގެފާނުގެ އިރާދަފުޅު އުޑުގައި ފުޅުވާ ފަދައިން ބިމުގައިވެސް ފުޅުވާށިއެވެ.

**6:11**

އަޅަމެންނަށް މިއަދު ބޭނުންވާ ކާނާ މިއަދު ދެއްވާށިއެވެ.

**6:12**

އަދި އަޅަމެންނަށް ކުށްކުރި މީހުންނަށް އަޅަމެން މާފުކުރާ ފަދައިން އަޅަމެންގެ ކުށްތަކަށް މާފުކޮށްދެއްވާށިއެވެ.

**6:13**

އަދި ތިޔަބައިމީހުން މަގުފުރައްދާ ކަންތަކަށް އަޅަމެން ނުގެންދަވާށިއެވެ. އަދި ނުބައިކަމުން އަޅަމެން ސަލާމަތްކޮށްދެއްވާށިއެވެ. އާމީން.

# DUTCH

Schrift
Matteüs 6:9–13

6:9
Bid daarom op deze manier: Onze Vader die in de hemel zijt, uw naam worde geheiligd.

6:10
Uw koninkrijk kome. Uw wil geschiede op aarde, zoals in de hemel.

6:11
Geef ons heden ons dagelijks brood.

6:12
En vergeef ons onze schulden, zoals wij onze schuldenaren vergeven.

6:13
En leid ons niet in verzoeking, maar verlos ons van het kwade: want van U is het koninkrijk, en de kracht, en de glorie, voor altijd. Amen.

# ENGLISH

Scripture
Matthew 6:9–13

6:9
After this manner therefore pray ye: Our Father which art in heaven, Hallowed be thy name.

6:10
Thy kingdom come. Thy will be done in earth, as it is in heaven.

6:11
Give us this day our daily bread.

6:12
And forgive us our debts, as we forgive our debtors.

6:13
And lead us not into temptation, but deliver us from evil: For thine is the kingdom, and the power, and the glory, for ever. Amen.

# ESTONIAN

Pühakiri
Matteuse 6:9–13

6:9
Palvetage siis nii: Meie Isa, kes sa oled taevas, pühitsetud olgu Sinu nimi.

6:10
Sinu kuningriik tulgu. Sinu tahtmine sündigu maa peal nagu taevas.

6:11
Anna meile täna meie igapäevane leib.

6:12
Ja anna meile andeks meie võlad, nagu meie anname andeks oma võlglastele.

6:13
Ja ära saada meid kiusatusse, vaid päästa meid kurjast, sest Sinu päralt on kuningriik ja vägi ja au igavesti. Aamen.

# EWE

Dɔŋlɔ Kɔkɔe
Mateo 6:9–13

6:9
Eya ta mido gbe ɖa le mɔ sia nu bena: Mía Fofo, si le dzifo,
Wò ŋkɔ nakɔ!

6:10
Wò fiaɖufe nava. Wò lɔlɔ̃nu nava eme le anyigba dzi, abe ale si
wòle le dzifo ene.

6:11
Na míafe gbesiagbenuɖuɖu mí egbea.

6:12
Eye nàtsɔ míafe fewo ke mí, abe ale si míetsɔa míafe fenyilawo
kea mí ene.

6:13
Eye mègakplɔ mí yi tetekpɔ me o, ke boŋ ɖe mí tso vɔ̃ me, Elabena
tɔwòe nye Fiaɖufe la kple ŋusẽ kple ŋutikɔkɔe tegbee. Amen.

# FINNISH

Raamattu
Matteus 6:9–13

6:9
Rukoilkaa siis näin: Isä meidän, joka olet taivaassa, pyhitetty olkoon sinun nimesi.

6:10
Tulkoon sinun valtakuntasi. Tapahtukoon Sinun tahtosi maan päällä niinkuin taivaassa.

6:11
Anna meille tänä päivänä meidän jokapäiväinen leipämme.

6:12
Ja anna meille anteeksi meidän velkamme, niin kuin mekin annamme anteeksi velallisillemme.

6:13
Älä saata meitä kiusaukseen, vaan päästä meidät pahasta, sillä sinun on valtakunta ja voima ja kunnia iankaikkisesti. Aamen.

# FRENCH

Écriture
Matthieu 6:9–13

6:9
Priez donc de cette manière: Notre Père qui es aux cieux, que ton nom soit sanctifié.

6:10
Que ton règne vienne. Que ta volonté soit faite sur la terre comme au ciel.

6:11
Donne-nous aujourd'hui notre pain quotidien.

6:12
Et pardonne-nous nos dettes, comme nous remettons à nos débiteurs.

6:13
Et ne nous soumets pas à la tentation, mais délivre-nous du mal : car c'est à toi qu'appartiennent le royaume, la puissance et la gloire, pour toujours. Amen.

# FRISIAN

Skrift
Mattéus 6:9–13

6:9
Sa bidde jimme dêrom: Us Heit, dy't yn 'e himelen binne, hillige wurde jins namme.

6:10
Komme dyn keninkryk. Jo wil wurdt dien op ierde, lykas yn 'e himel.

6:11
Jou ús hjoed ús deistich brea.

6:12
En ferjou ús ús skulden, lykas wy ús skuldners ferjaan.

6:13
En lied ús net yn fersiking, mar ferlos ús fan 'e kweade: Hwent dyn is it keninkryk, en de macht en de hearlikheid, foar altyd. Amen.

# GALICIAN

Escritura
Mateo 6:9–13

6:9
Rezades deste xeito: Pai noso que estás nos ceos, santificado sexa o teu nome.

6:10
Veña o teu reino. Fágase a túa vontade na terra, como no ceo.

6:11
Dános hoxe o noso pan de cada día.

6:12
E perdoa-nos as nosas débedas, como nós perdoamos aos nosos debedores.

6:13
E non nos deixes caer na tentación, senón líbranos do mal: porque teu é o reino, o poder e a gloria para sempre. Amén.

# GEORGIAN

წმინდა წერილი
მათე 6:9–13

6:9
ასე ილოცეთ: მამაო ჩვენო, რომელიც ხარ ზეცაში, წმიდა იყოს სახელი შენი.

6:10
მოვიდეს შენი სამეფო. იყოს შენი ნება დედამიწაზე, როგორც ზეცაში.

6:11
მოგვეც დღეს ჩვენი ყოველდღიური პური.

6:12
და მოგვიტევე ჩვენი ვალი, როგორც ჩვენ ვაპატიებთ ჩვენს მოვალეებს.

6:13
და ნუ შეგვიყვან ჩვენ განსაცდელში, არამედ გვიხსენი ბოროტებისგან, რადგან შენია სასუფეველი და ძალა და დიდება მარადიულად. ამინ.

# GERMAN

6:9
Nach dieser Art beten Sie daher: Unser Vater, die Kunst im Himmel, heiligt, ist dein Name.

6:10
Euer Königreich komme. Dein Wille wird in der Erde gemacht, wie es im Himmel ist.

6:11
Gib uns heute unser tägliches Brot.

6:12
Und vergib uns unsere Schulden, wenn wir unseren Schuldnern verzeihen.

6:13
Und führen uns nicht in Versuchung, sondern richten Sie uns vom Bösen ab: Denn Ihr ist das Königreich und die Kraft und die Herrlichkeit für immer. Amen.

# GREEK

Γραφή
Ματθαίος 6:9–13

6:9
Με αυτόν τον τρόπο προσευχηθείτε λοιπόν: Πατέρα μας που είσαι στους ουρανούς, να αγιαστεί το όνομά σου.

6:10
Ελθέτω η βασιλεία σου. Γίνεται το θέλημά σου στη γη, όπως στον ουρανό.

6:11
Δώσε μας σήμερα το καθημερινό μας ψωμί.

6:12
Και συγχώρησέ μας τα χρέη μας, όπως συγχωρούμε εμείς τους οφειλέτες μας.

6:13
Και μη μας οδηγήσεις σε πειρασμό, αλλά λύτρωσέ μας από το κακό· γιατί δική σου είναι η βασιλεία και η δύναμη και η δόξα στον αιώνα. Αμήν.

# GUARANI

Escritura
Mateo 6:9–13

6:9
Peñembo'e péicha: Ore Ru yvágape reimeva, toñemomarangatu nde réra.

6:10
Nde rréino toju. Tojejapo ne rembipota ko yvy ape ári, yvágape ojejapoháicha.

6:11
Eme'ẽ oréve ko árape ore mbujape ára ha ára.

6:12
Ha oreperdona ore deuvéva, ore roperdonaháicha ore odevévape.

6:13
Ani oregueraha jepy'ara'ãme, orepe'a uvei mba'evaígui. Amén.

# GUJARATI

શાસ્ત્ર
માત્થી ૬:૯-૧૩


**6:9**
આ રીતે પ્રાર્થના કર્યા પછી તમે પ્રાર્થના કરો: આપણો બાપ, જે આકાશમાં કળા કરે છે, તે પવિત્ર તારું નામ છે.

**6:10**
તારું સામ્રાજ્ય આવે છે. જેમ આકાશમાં છે તેમ પૃથ્વીમાં પણ તારું થશે.

**6:11**
આ દિવસે અમારી રોજની રોટલી અમને આપ.

**6:12**
અને જેમ આપણે આપણા દેવાદારોને માફ કરીએ છીએ તેમ આપણું ઋણ માફ કરજો.

**6:13**
અને અમને લાલચમાં ન લાવો. પણ અમને દુષ્ટતાથી મુક્ત કરો. શા માટે? કારણ કે રાજ્ય, પરાક્રમ અને મહિમા સદાને માટે તારું જ છે. આમીન.

# HAITIAN CREOLE

Ekriti yo
Matye 6:9–13

6:9
Se poutèt sa, priye konsa: Papa nou ki nan syèl la, se pou non w sen.

6:10
Wi wayòm ou an vini. Se volonte w ki fèt sou tè a, menm jan li fèt nan syèl la.

6:11
Jòdi a, ban nou pen nou chak jou.

6:12
Epi padonnen dèt nou yo, menm jan nou padonnen dèt nou yo.

6:13
Pa lage nou nan tantasyon, men delivre nou anba sa ki mal. Amèn.

# HAUSA

Nassi
Matiyu 6:9–13

6:9
Ta haka sai ku yi addu'a: Ubanmu wanda ke cikin Sama, A tsarkake sunanka.

6:10
Mulkinka ya zo. A aikata nufinka cikin duniya, kamar yadda ake yinsa cikin sama.

6:11
Ka ba mu wannan rana abincinmu na yau da kullun.

6:12
Kuma Ka gafarta mana basusukan mu, kamar yadda muke gafarta wa ma'abuta bashi.

6:13
Kada ka kai mu cikin jaraba, amma ka cece mu daga mugunta: gama mulki naka ne, da iko, da ɗaukaka, har abada abadin. Amin.

# HEBREW

שדוקה יבתכ
מתי 6:9-13

6:9
לפי כד התפללו: אביו אשר בשמים, יתקדש שמך.

6:10
בוא מלכותך. יעשה רצונך כאראק ומכ בשמים.

6:11
תן לנו והיה םיוה תא לחמנו היומי.

6:12
וסלח לנו על וה בוחותינו וכש שאנו סולחים לחייבינו.

6:13
ואל תביא אותנו לפיתוי, אלא הצילנו מרע: כי שלך המלכות וההוכח התהילה
לעולם עד. אמן.

# HINDI

धर्मग्रंथ
मैथ्यू 6:9–13

6:9

इस प्रकार तुम प्रार्थना करो: हे हमारे पिता, जो स्वर्ग में है, तेरा नाम पवित्र माना जाए।

6:10

तुम्हारा राज्य आए। तेरी इच्छा जैसे स्वर्ग में पूरी होती है, वैसे ही पृथ्वी पर भी पूरी हो।

6:11

आज हमें हमारी प्रतिदिन की रोटी दो।

6:12

और हमारे कर्ज़ माफ करो, जैसे हम अपने कर्ज़दारों को माफ करते हैं।

6:13

और हमें परीक्षा में न ला, परन्तु बुराई से बचा; क्योंकि राज्य और सामर्थ, और महिमा सदैव तेरी ही है। आमीन.

# HMONG

Vajluskub
Mathais 6:9–13

6:9
Yog li ntawd, nej yuav tsum thov Vajtswv li no: Peb Leej Txiv uas
nyob saum ntuj ceeb tsheej, thov kom koj lub npe dawb huv.

6:10
Koj lub nceeg vaj tuaj. Koj lub siab yuav ua tiav hauv ntiaj teb,
ib yam li nws nyob saum ntuj.

6:11
Muab pub rau peb hnub no peb niaj hnub mov.

6:12
Thiab zam txim rau peb cov nuj nqis, ib yam li peb zam peb
cov nuj nqis.

6:13
Thiab tsis txhob coj peb mus rau hauv kev ntxias, tab sis cawm
peb ntawm kev phem: Rau koj lub nceeg vaj, thiab lub hwj
chim, thiab lub yeeb koob, mus ib txhis. Amen.

# HUNGARIAN

Szentírás
Máté 6:9–13

6:9
Így imádkozzatok tehát: Mi Atyánk, ki vagy a mennyekben, szenteltessék meg a te neved.

6:10
Jöjjön el a te országod. Legyen meg a te akaratod, amint a mennyben, úgy a földön is.

6:11
Add meg nekünk ma mindennapi kenyerünket.

6:12
És bocsásd meg az adósságainkat, ahogy mi is megbocsátunk az adósainknak.

6:13
És ne vígy minket kísértésbe, hanem szabadíts meg minket a gonosztól: Mert tiéd az ország, és a hatalom és a dics ség mindörökké. Ámen.

# IGBO

Akwụkwọ Nsọ
Matiu 6:9–13

## 6:9
Ya mere, kpenu ekpere otú a: Nna-ayi Nke bi n'elu-igwe, Ka edo aha-Gi nsọ.

## 6:10
Ala-eze-Gi bia. Ka eme uche-Gi n'uwa, dika esi eme n'elu-igwe.

## 6:11
Nye anyị nri ụbọchị taa.

## 6:12
Gbagharakwa anyị ụgwọ anyị ji, dị ka anyị na-agbaghara ndị ji anyị ụgwọ.

## 6:13
Eduba-kwa-la ayi n'ọnwunwa, ma naputa ayi n'aka ihe ọjọ: N'ihi na ala-eze bu Gi, na ike, na otuto, rue mbẹ ebighi-ebi. Amen.

# ICELANDIC

Ritningin
Matteusarguðspjall 6:9–13

6:9
Biðjið því: Faðir vor, faðir vor, þú sem ert á himnum, helgist þitt nafn.

6:10
Til komi þitt ríki. Verði þinn vilji á jörðu eins og á himni.

6:11
Gef oss í dag vort daglegt brauð.

6:12
Og fyrirgef oss vorar skuldir svo sem vér og fyrirgefum vorum skuldunautum.

6:13
Eigi leið þú oss í freistni heldur frelsa oss frá illu því að þitt er ríkið, mátturinn og dýrðin að eilífu. Amen.

# ILOCANO

Kasuratan
Mateo 6:9–13

**6:9**
Kastoy ngarud nga ikararagyo: Amami nga adda sadi langit, Nasantuan koma ti naganmo.

**6:10**
Umay ti pagariam. Maaramid koma ti pagayatam ditoy daga, kas iti maaramid idiay langit.

**6:11**
Itedmo kadakami ita nga aldaw ti tinapaymi iti inaldaw.

**6:12**
Ket pakawanennakami kadagiti utangmi, a kas iti panangpakawanmi kadagiti nakautang kadakami.

**6:13**
Ket saannakami nga iturong iti sulisog, no di ket ispalennakami iti dakes: Ta kukuam ti pagarian, ken ti pannakabalin, ken ti dayag, iti agnanayon. Amen.

# INDONESIAN

Kitab Suci
Matius 6:9–13

6:9
Karena itu berdoalah demikian: Bapa kami yang di surga,
Dikuduskanlah nama-Mu.

6:10
Datanglah kerajaan-Mu. Jadilah kehendak-Mu di bumi seperti
di surga.

6:11
Berikanlah kami pada hari ini makanan kami yang secukupnya.

6:12
Dan ampunilah kami akan hutang kami, seperti kami
mengampuni para debitur kami.

6:13
Dan janganlah membawa kami ke dalam pencobaan, tetapi
bebaskan kami dari yang jahat: Karena milikmu adalah
kerajaan, dan kekuatan, dan kemuliaan, untuk selama-
lamanya. Amin.

# IRISH

An Scrioptúr
Matha 6:9–13

6:9
Ar an modh seo guí dá bhrí sin: Ár nAthair atá ar neamh, Go naomhófar d'ainm.

6:10
Tigidh do ríocht. Déanfar do thoil ar talamh, mar a dhéantar ar neamh.

6:11
Tabhair dúinn inniu ár n-arán laethúil.

6:12
Agus maith dúinn ár bhfiacha, mar a mhaithimidne dár bhféichiúnaithe.

6:13
Agus ná leig i gcathú sinn, ach saor sinn ó olc: óir is leatsa an ríocht, agus an chumhacht, agus an ghlóir go brách. Amen.

# ITALIAN

Scrittura
Matteo 6:9–13


6:9
Voi dunque pregate così: Padre nostro che sei nei cieli, sia santificato il tuo nome.

6:10
Venga il tuo regno. Sia fatta la tua volontà come in cielo così in terra.

6:11
Dacci oggi il nostro pane quotidiano.

6:12
E rimetti a noi i nostri debiti, come noi li rimettiamo ai nostri debitori.

6:13
E non indurci in tentazione, ma liberaci dal male: perché tuo è il regno, la potenza e la gloria per sempre. Amen.

# JAPANESE

経典
マタイ 6:9–13

6:9
したがって、この方法の後で、あなたがたは祈ってください： 天におられ
る私たちの父よ、あなたの御名が崇められますように。

6:10
あなたの王国が来ますように。 あなたの御心が天で行われるように、
地でも行われます。

6:11
この日、私たちに日々の糧を与えてください。

6:12
そして、私たちが債務者を赦すように、私たちの負債も赦して
ください。

6:13
そして私たちを誘惑に導かないで、悪から救い出してください。王国と
力と栄光は永遠にあなたのものだからです。 アーメン。

# KAZAKH

Қасиетті жазу
Матай 6:9–13


6:9
Осылайша, сенімен бірге дұға етіңдер: көктегі Әкеміздің аты-жөні, сенің есіміңе алынды.

6:10
Сенің Патшалығы келді. Сенің көкте болғандай, сенің жерлеріңде болады.

6:11
Бізге бұл күні күнделікті нан беріңіз.

6:12
Біздің қарыздарымызды кешір, борышкерлерімізді кешіреміз.

6:13
Және бізді азғыруға алып келмейді, бірақ бізді зұлымдықтан құтқарыңыз: өйткені сендер - Патшалық, билік пен даңқ, мәңгі. Аумин.

# KHMER

បទគម្ពីរ
ម៉ាថាយ ៦:៩-១៣

៦:៩
ដូច្នេះ     ចូរអ្នក‍រាល់គ្នានាអធិស្ឋានតាមរបៀបនេះថា     ៖
ព្រះវរបិតានៃយើងខ្ញុំដែលគង់នៅស្ថានសួគ៌អើយ សូមឱ្យ
ព្រះនាមទ្រង់បានបរិសុទ្ធ។

៦:១០
ព្រះរាជាណាចក្ររបស់អ្នកមក។  ព្រះហប្ញទ័យទ្រង់បានសម្រេច
នៅលើផែនដី ដូចនៅស្ថានសួគ៌ដែរ។

៦:១១
ផុតល់ឱ្យយើងនៅថ្ងៃនេះនូវនំបុ័ងបរ្‍ចាំថ្ងៃរបស់យើង។

៦:១២
ហើយអត់ទោសឱ្យយើងនូវបំណុលរបស់យើងដូចដែលយើងអ
ត់ទោសឱ្យកូនបំណុលរបស់យើង។

៦:១៣
ហើយកុំនាំយើងទៅក្នុងការល្បួងឡើយ  ប៉ុន្តែសូមរំដោះ
យើងខ្ញុំឱ្យរួចពីសេចក្ដីអាក្រក់ចុះ     ដ្បិតទ្រង់ជាព្រះ
រាជាណាចក្រ ឫទ្ធានុភាព និងសិរីល្អអស់រៀងរហូត។ អាម៉ែន។

# KINYARWANDA

Ibyanditswe Byera
Matayo 6:9–13

6:9
Nyuma y'ubu buryo rero musenge: Data wa twese uri mu ijuru, izina ryawe ryubahwe.

6:10
Ingoma yawe iraza. Ibyo ushaka bikorwe mu isi, nk'uko biri mu ijuru.

6:11
Duhe uyu munsi imigati yacu ya buri munsi.

6:12
Kandi utubabarire imyenda yacu, nkuko tubabarira abadufitiye imyenda.

6:13
Ntutuyobore mu bishuko, ahubwo udukize ikibi: Kuko ubwami bwawe, n'imbaraga n'icyubahiro cyawe iteka ryose. Amen.

# KOREAN

성경
마태복음 6:9-13

6:9
그러므로 이와 같이 너희에게 기도하라 하늘에 계신 우리
아버지여 이름이 거룩히 여김을 받으시오며

6:10
당신의 왕국이 임하옵소서. 뜻이 하늘에서 이룬 것 같이 땅에서도
이루어지이다.

6:11
오늘 우리에게 일용할 양식을 주소서.

6:12
우리가 우리에게 죄 지은 자를 사하여 준 것 같이 우리 죄를
사하여 주옵시고

6:13
우리를 시험에 들게 하지 마옵시고 다만 악에서 구하옵소서
나라와 권세와 영광이 영원토록 아버지께 있나이다 아멘.

# KRIO

Skripcho
Matyu 6:9–13


6:9
So una pre fɔ se: Wi Papa we de na ɛvin, mek yu nem oli."

6:10
Yu kiŋdɔm kam. Mek wetin yu want bi na dis wɔl, jɔs lɛk aw i de bi na ɛvin.

6:11
Gi wi dis de wi it fɔ ɛvride.

6:12
Ɛn fɔgiv wi di dɛt dɛn, jɔs lɛk aw wi de fɔgiv di wan dɛn we gɛt dɛt.

6:13
Ɛn nɔ lid wi pan tɛmteshɔn, bɔt sev wi frɔm bad, bikɔs na yu gɛt di Kiŋdɔm, di pawa, ɛn di glori sote go. Amen.

# KURMANJI

Nivîsara Pîroz
Metta 6:9–13

6:9
Ji ber vê yekê hûn bi vî awayî dua bikin: Bavê me yê li ezmanan, navê te pîroz be.

6:10
Padî ahiya te bê. Daxwaza te, çawa ku li ezmanan e, li erdê jî be.

6:11
Nanê me yê rojane bide vê rojê.

6:12
Û çawa ku em deyndarên xwe dibihûrin, deynê me jî bibihûre.

6:13
Û me neke nav ceribandinê, lê me ji xerabiyê xilas bike: Çimkî Padî ahiya, hêz û rûmeta her û her ya te ne. Amîn.

# SORANI

کتێبی پیرۆز
مەتتا ٦: ٩ـ١٣

## 6:9

بۆیە بەم شێوەیە دوعا بکەن: باوکمان کە لە ئاسمانیت، وا، ناوت پیرۆز بێت.

## ٦:١٠
کاتژمێری

با نۆچ کەوە، هەوا بێتە ئارای، ویستی تۆ لەسەر هەوزی یوی بێتە ئارای، کەوە نۆچ لە شانشینی تۆ وەرە. وەک لە ئاسمان.

## 6:11
ئەمڕۆ ڕۆژە نانی ڕۆژانەمان پێ ببدە.

## 6:12
وە لە قەرزەکانمان خۆشبە، وەک چۆن ئێمەی لە قەرزدارەکانمان خۆش دەبین.

## 6:13
مەهێڵە بکەوینە تاقیکردنەوە، هەڵمان لە خراپەکار بگەرامان بکە، چونکە شانشینی و دەسەڵات و شکۆمەندیی بۆ تۆیە. ئامین.

55

# KYRGYZ

Ыйык Жазуу
Матай 6:9–13

6:9
Ошондуктан мындай деп сыйынгыла: Асмандагы Атабыз, сенин ысымың ыйыкталсын.

6:10
Сенин падышачылыгың келсин. Сенин эркиң асмандагыдай эле жерде да аткарылат.

6:11
Ушул күнү бизге күнүмдүк наныбызды бер.

6:12
Биз карыздарыбызды кечиргендей, биздин карыздарыбызды да кечир.

6:13
Бизди азгырууга алып барба, бизди жамандыктан куткар, анткени Падышалык, күч жана даңк түбөлүккө Сеники. Оомийин.

# LAO

ພຣະຄຳພີ
ມັດທາຍ 6:9–13


6:9
ດ້ວຍນັ້ນ ເຈົ້າຈົ່ງອະທິຖານດ້ວນີ້: ພຣະບິດາຂອງພວກເຮົາຜູ້ສະຖິດຢູ່ໃນ
ສະຫວັນ, ຂໍໃຫ້ພຣະນາມຂອງພຣະອົງເປັນທີ່ສັກສິດ.

6:10
ອານາຈັກຂອງເຈົ້າມາ. ຄວາມປະສົງຂອງເຈົ້າຈະຖືກເຮັດຢູ່ໃນແຜ່ນດິນ
ໂລກ, ຄືກັບຢູ່ໃນສະຫວັນ.

6:11
ໃຫ້ພວກເຮົາເຈົ້າຈີ່ປະຈຳວັນຂອງພວກເຮົາໃນມື້ນີ້.

6:12
ແລະຍົກໂທດໃຫ້ພວກເຮົາເປັນໜີ້ຂອງພວກເຮົາ, ດັ່ງທີ່ພວກເຮົາໃຫ້ອະ
ໄພລູກໜີ້ຂອງພວກເຮົາ.

6:13
ແລະບໍ່ໃຫ້ພວກເຮົາເຈົ້າໄປໃນການລໍ້ລວງ, ແຕ່ບໍດບ່ອຍພວກເຮົາຈາກ
ຄວາມຊົ່ວຮ້າຍ: ສຳລັບພຣະອົງເປັນອານາຈັກ, ແລະອຳນາດ, ແລະລັດສະ
ໝີພາບ, ຕະຫຼອດໄປ. ອາແມນ.

# LATIN

Scriptura
Matthew 6:9–13

6:9
Sic ergo vos orate: Pater noster, qui es in caelis, sanctificetur nomen tuum.

6:10
Adveniat regnum tuum. Fiat voluntas tua, sicut in coelo, in terra.

6:11
Panem nostrum quotidianum da nobis hodie.

6:12
Et dimitte nobis debita nostra, sicut dimittimus debitoribus nostris.

6:13
Et ne nos inducas in tentationem, sed libera nos a malo. Amen.

# LATVIAN

Sv tie Raksti
Mateja 6:9–13

6:9
T p c l dziet š di: T vs m su, kas esi debes s, sv t ts lai top Tavs v rds.

6:10
Lai n k Tava valst ba. Tavs pr ts lai notiek virs zemes, t pat k debes s.

6:11
Dod mums šodien m su dieniš o maizi.

6:12
Un piedod mums m su par dus, k m s piedodam saviem par dniekiem.

6:13
Un neieved m s k rdin šan , bet atpest m s no auna, jo Tava ir valst ba un sp ks un gods m ž gi. men.

# LITHUANIAN

Raštas
Mato 6:9–13

6:9
Tod l melskit s taip: T ve m s , kuris esi danguje, teb nie
šventas tavo vardas.

6:10
Teateina Tavo karalyst . Tavo valia teb nie žem je, kaip
danguje.

6:11
Kasdien s duonos duok mums šiandien.

6:12
Ir atleisk mums m s skolas, kaip ir mes atleidžiame savo
skolininkams.

6:13
Ir nevesk m s pagund , bet gelb k mus nuo blogio, nes
Tavo yra karalyst , j ga ir šlov per amžius. Amen.

# LUXEMBOURGISH

Schrëft
Matthäus 6:9–13


6:9
No dëser Aart a Weis also biede Dir: Eise Papp, deen am Himmel ass, Gehellegt ginn Ären Numm.

6:10
Däi Räich komm. Däi Wëlle geschéien op der Äerd, wéi et am Himmel ass.

6:11
Gëff eis haut eist deeglecht Brout.

6:12
A verzei eis eis Scholden, wéi mir eis Scholden verzeien.

6:13
A féiert eis net an d'Versuchung, mä befreit eis vum Béisen: Fir Däin ass d'Kinnekräich an d'Muecht an d'Herrlechkeet fir ëmmer. Amen.

# MACEDONIAN

Светото писмо
Матеј 6:9–13

6:9
Затоа молете се вака: Оче наш, Кој си на небесата, да се свети
името Твое.

6:10
Да дојде царството твое. Да биде волјата Твоја на земјата,
како и на небото.

6:11
Дај ни го денес нашиот секојдневен леб.

6:12
И прости ни ги долговите наши, како што ние им простуваме
на нашите должници.

6:13
И не воведувај нè во искушение, туку избави нè од злото, зашто
Твое е царството и силата и славата засекогаш. Амин.

# MAITHILI

शास्त्र

मत्ती 6:9–13

6:9 मे

तैँ अहाँ सभ एहि तरहेँ प्रार्थना करू, "हे हमर सभक पिता जे स्‍वर्ग मे छी, अहाँक नाम पवित्र होअय।"

6:10 मे

तोहर राज्य आऊ। जेना स्वर्ग मे होइत अछि तहिना पृथ्वी पर सेहो अहाँक इच्छा पूरा हो।

6:11 मे

आइ हमरा सभकेँ अपन रोजक रोटी दिअ।

6:12 मे

आ हमरा सभक ऋण क्षमा करू, जेना हम सभ अपन ऋणी केँ क्षमा कैरत छी।

6:13 मे

आ हमरा सभ केँ परीक्षा मे नहि लऽ जाउ, बल्‍कि हमरा सभ केँ अधलाह सँ बचाउ। आमीन।

# MALAGASY

Soratra Masina
Matio 6:9–13

6:9
Koa mivavaha toy izao ianareo: Rainay Izay any an-danitra, hohamasinina anie ny anaranao.

6:10
Ho tonga anie ny fanjakanao. Hatao anie ny sitraponao ety an-tany tahaka ny any an-danitra.

6:11
Omeo anay anio izay hanina sahaza ho anay.

6:12
Ary mamelà ny helokay, tahaka ny namelanay izay meloka taminay.

6:13
Ary aza mitondra anay ho amin' ny fakam-panahy, fa manafaha anay amin' ny ratsy; fa Anao ny fanjakana sy ny hery ary ny voninahitra mandrakizay. Amen.

# MALAY

Kitab Suci
Matius 6:9–13

6:9
Karena itu berdoalah demikian: Bapa kami yang di sorga, Dikuduskanlah nama-Mu.

6:10
Datanglah kerajaan-Mu. Jadilah kehendak-Mu di bumi seperti di sorga.

6:11
Berilah kami pada hari ini makanan kami yang secukupnya.

6:12
Dan ampunilah kami akan hutang kami, sebagaimana kami juga mengampuni orang yang berhutang kepada kami.

6:13
Dan janganlah membawa kami ke dalam pencobaan, tetapi lepaskanlah kami daripada yang jahat: Sebab Engkaulah yang empunya Kerajaan dan kuasa dan kemuliaan sampai selama-lamanya. Amin.

# MALAYALAM

വിശുദ്ധ ഗ്രന്ഥം
മത്തായി 6:9–13

6:9
ഇപ്രകാരം പ്രാർത്ഥിക്കുക:
സ്വർഗ്ഗസ്ഥനായ ഞങ്ങളുടെ പിതാവേ,
നിന്റെനാമം വിശുദ്ധീകരിക്കപ്പടെണേമേ.

6:10
നിന്റെ രാജ്യം വരണേമേ. നിന്റെ ഇഷ്ടം
സ്വർഗ്ഗത്തിലനെന്നപോലെ ഭൂമിയിലും
ആകണേമേ.

6:11
ഞങ്ങളുടെദൈനെംദിനഅപ്പംഞങ്ങൾക്ക്
തരണേമേ.

6:12
ഞങ്ങളുടെ കടക്കാരോട് ഞങ്ങൾ
ക്ഷമിക്കുന്നതുപോലെ ഞങ്ങളുടെ
കടങ്ങളും ഞങ്ങളോടും ക്ഷമിക്കണേമേ.

6:13
ഞങ്ങളെ പ്രലോഭനത്തിലകേക്ക്
നയിക്കരുത്, തിന്മയിൽ നിന്ന്
ഞങ്ങളെ വിടുവിക്കണേമേ: രാജ്യവും
ശക്തിയും മഹത്വവും എന്നനേക്കും
നിനക്കുള്ളതാകുന്നു. ആമേൻ.

66

# MALTESE

Iskrittura
Mattew 6:9–13

6:9
Balhekk itolbu intom: Missierna li int fis-smewwiet, Imqaddes ismek.

6:10
Ejja saltnatek. Issir ir-rieda tieghek fl-art, kif inhi fis-sema.

6:11
Aghtina llum il-hob taghna ta' kuljum.

6:12
U ahfrilna d-djun taghna, bhalma ahna nahfru lid-debitur taghna.

6:13
U twasslux fit-tentazzjoni, imma ehlisna mill-ha en: Ghax tieghek huma s-saltna, u l-qawwa u l-glorja, ghal dejjem. Ammen.

# MAORI

Karaipiture
Mataio 6:9–13

6:9
Na kia penei ta koutou inoi: E to matou Matua i te rangi, Kia tapu tou ingoa.

6:10
Kia tae mai tou rangatiratanga. Kia meatia tau e pai ai ki runga ki te whenua, kia rite ano ki to te rangi.

6:11
Homai ki a matou aianei he taro ma matou mo tenei ra.

6:12
Murua o matou hara, me matou hoki e muru nei i te hunga e hara mai ana ki a matou.

6:13
Aua hoki matou e kawea kia whakawaia, engari whakaorangia matou i te kino: Nou hoki te rangatiratanga, te kaha, me te kororia, ake ake. Amine.

# MARATHI

धर्मशास्त्र

मत्तय ६:९-१३

6:9

अशा रीतीने तुम्ही प्रार्थना करा: आमचा पिता जो स्वर्गात आहे, तो तुझे नाव पवित्र असावा.

6:10

तुझे राज्य येते. तुझी इच्छा जशी स्वर्गात आहे तशीच पृथ्वीवरही केली जाईल.

6:11

या दिवशी आम्हाला आमची रोजची भाकरी द्या.

6:12

आणि आमचे कर्ज माफ करा, जसे आम्ही आमच्या कर्जदारांना क्षमा करतो.

6:13

आणि आम्हांला प्रलोभनात घेऊन जाऊ नका, तर दुष्टेपासून आपली सुटका करा: कारण तुझे राज्य, सामर्थ्य आणि वैभव कायमचे आहे.

# MONGOLIAN

Судар
Матай 6:9–13

6:9
Иймээс та нар ингэж залбир: Тэнгэр дэх Эцэг минь ээ, Таны нэр ариусгагдах болтугай.

6:10
Таны хаанчлал ирэгтүн. Таны хүсэл тэнгэрт байгаа шиг газар дээр биелнэ.

6:11
Өнөөдөр бидний өдөр тутмын талхыг бидэнд өгөөч.

6:12
Бид өртэй хүмүүсээ уучилсны адил бидний өрийг өршөөгөөч.

6:13
Биднийг уруу таталтанд бүү оруулаач, харин биднийг бузар муугаас авраач: Учир нь хаант улс, хүч чадал, алдар суу үүрд чинийх юм. Амен.

# NEPALI

धर्मशास्त्र

मत्ती ६:९-१३

6:9

यसकारण तिमीहरू प्रार्थना गर: हे हाम्रा पिता, जो स्वर्गमा हुनुहुन्छ, तपाईंको नाउँ पवित्र होस्।

6:10

तपाईंको राज्य आओस्। तपाईंको इच्छा स्वर्गमा जस्तै पृथ्वीमा पनि पूरा हुनेछ।

6:11

आज हामीलाई हाम्रो दैनिक रोटी दिनुहोस्।

6:12

अनि हाम्रा ऋणीहरूलाई क्षमा गरेझैं हाम्रा ऋणहरू पनि क्षमा गर।

6:13

अनि हामीलाई परीक्षामा नलैजानु होस्। तर हामीलाई दुष्टताबाट बचाउनुहोस्। किनभने राज्य, शक्ति र महिमा सदा-सर्वदा तपाईंकै हो। आमीन।

# NORWEGIAN

Bibelen
Matteus 6:9–13

6:9
På denne måten ber dere derfor: Fader vår, som er i himmelen, helliget bli ditt navn.

6:10
Kom ditt rike. Skje din vilje på jorden, som i himmelen.

6:11
Gi oss i dag vårt daglige brød.

6:12
Og tilgi oss vår skyld, som vi tilgir våre skyldnere.

6:13
Og led oss ikke inn i fristelse, men fri oss fra det onde: For ditt er riket og makten og æren i all evighet. Amen.

# OROMO

Caaffata Qulqullaa'oo
Maatewos 6:9–13


6:9
Kanaaf akkasitti kadhadhaa: Yaa Abbaa keenya isa samii irra
jirtu, Maqaan kee haa qulqullaa'u!

6:10
Mootummaan kee kottu. Fedhiin kee akkuma samii irratti
raawwatamu lafa irrattis haa raawwatamu.

6:11
Guyyaa har'aa buddeena keenya guyyaa guyyaa nuuf kenni.

6:12
Akkuma nuti warra liqii keenyaaf dhiifama goonu, liqii keenyas
nuuf dhiisi.

6:13
Mootummaan, aangoon, ulfinnis bara baraan kan kee waan
ta'eef, hamaa irraa nu baasi malee, qorumsatti nu hin galchiin.
Ameen.

# PASHTO

انجیل
متی 6: 9-13


6:9

هل دي طريقي ورسوسته تاس دعا وكرئ: زمورو پلار چي په آسمان كي دي،
ستا نوم دي مقدس وي.


6:10

ستا سلطنت راشي. ستا اراده په زمكه كي پوره هغه کيريدي لكه هغنگه
چي په آسمان كي ده.


6:11

نن ورځ مورو ته زمورو ورځنی ډوډی راكړه.


6:12–13

او مورو ته زمورو قرضونه معاف كړه هغه لكه هغنگه چي مورو هم پخپل روپ
ورکوونکي معاف کړل.
او مورو په آزميښت كي مه خار، خو له بده خخ وژغوره: خكه چي
پاچاهي، قدرت او جلال د تل لپاره ستا دي. آمین

# POLISH

Pismo
Mateusza 6:9–13

6:9
Po tej drodze módlcie si  wi c: Ojcze nasz, który jest w
niebie, wi  si  imi  Twoje.

6:10
Przyjd  królestwo Twoje. B d  wola Twoja jako w niebie, tak
i na ziemi.

6:11
Chleba naszego powszedniego daj nam dzisiaj.

6:12
I przebacz nam nasze winy, tak jak my odpuszczamy naszym
winowajcom.

6:13
I nie wód  nas na pokuszenie, ale nas zbaw od złego, bo Twoje
jest królestwo i moc, i chwała, na wieki. Amen.

# PORTUGUESE

Escritura
Mateus 6:9–13

6:9
Portanto, orai assim: Pai nosso, que estás nos céus, santificado seja o teu nome.

6:10
Venha o teu reino. Seja feita a tua vontade assim na terra como no céu.

6:11
O pão nosso de cada dia dá-nos hoje.

6:12
E perdoa-nos as nossas dívidas, assim como nós perdoamos aos nossos devedores.

6:13
E não nos deixes cair em tentação, mas livra-nos do mal: Porque teu é o reino, e o poder, e a glória, para sempre. Amém.

# PUNJABI

ਪੋਥੀ
ਮੱਤੀ 6:9–13

6:9
ਇਸ ਲਈ ਇਸ ਤਰ੍ਹਾਂ ਪ੍ਰਾਰਥਨਾ ਕਰੋ: ਸਾਡੇ ਪਿਤਾ ਜੋ ਸਵਰਗ ਵਿੱਚ ਹੈ,
ਤੇਰਾ ਨਾਮ ਪਵਿੱਤਰ ਮੰਨਿਆ ਜਾਵੇ।

6:10
ਤੇਰਾ ਰਾਜ ਆਵੇ। ਤੇਰੀ ਮਰਜ਼ੀ ਧਰਤੀ ਉੱਤੇ ਪੂਰੀ ਹੋਵੇ, ਜਿਵੇਂ ਸਵਰਗ
ਵਿੱਚ ਹੁੰਦੀ ਹੈ।

6:11
ਸਾਨੂੰ ਅੱਜ ਸਾਡੀ ਰੋਜ਼ ਦੀ ਰੋਟੀ ਦੇਹ।

6:12
ਅਤੇ ਸਾਡੇ ਕਰਜ਼ ਮਾਫ਼ ਕਰ, ਜਿਵੇਂ ਅਸੀਂ ਆਪਣੇ ਕਰਜ਼ਦਾਰਾਂ ਨੂੰ ਮਾਫ਼ ਕਰ।

6:13
ਅਤੇ ਸਾਨੂੰ ਪਰਤਾਵੇ ਵਿੱਚ ਨਾ ਲੈ, ਪਰ ਸਾਨੂੰ ਬੁਰਾਈ ਤੋਂ ਬਚਾਓ: ਰਾਜ,
ਸ਼ਕਤੀ ਅਤੇ ਮਹਿਮਾ ਸਦਾ ਲਈ ਤੇਰੀ ਹੈ. ਆਮੀਨ।

# QUECHUA

Qelqa
Mateo 6:9–13

6:9
Chay hinaqa, kay hinata mañakuychis: Hanaq pachapi kaq Yayayku, sutiyki ch'uyanchasqa kachun, nispa.

6:10
Reinoyki hamuy. Munayniyki kay pachapipas rurasqa kachun, hanaq pachapi hina.

6:11
Kunan punchaw sapa punchaw mikuyniykuta quwayku.

6:12
Huchaykutapas pampachawayku, imaynan noqaykupas manukuwaqniykuta pampachayku hinata.

6:13
Ama wateqayman pusawaykuchu, aswanqa mana allinmanta kacharichiwayku. Amen.

# ROMANIAN

Scriptura
Matei 6:9–13

6:9
De aceea, rugaţi-v  astfel: Tat l nostru care eşti în ceruri,
sfinţit-se numele T u.

6:10
Vie împ r ţia Ta. Fac -se voia Ta pe p mânt, aşa cum este
în ceruri.

6:11
D -ne ast zi pâinea noastr  cea de toate zilele.

6:12
Şi ne iart  nou  datoriile, precum şi noi iert m pe datornicii
noştri.

6:13
Şi nu ne duce în ispit , ci izb veşte-ne de r u, c ci a Ta este
împ r ţia, puterea şi slava în vecii vecilor. Amin.

# RUSSIAN

Священное писание
Матфея 6:9–13

6:9
Итак, молитесь: Отче наш, сущий на небесах, да святится имя Твое.

6:10
Да приидет Царствие Твое. Да будет воля Твоя на земле, как на небе.

6:11
Хлеб наш насущный дай нам на сей день.

6:12
И прости нам долги наши, как мы прощаем должникам нашим.

6:13
И не введи нас во искушение, но избавь нас от лукавого, ибо Твое есть Царство, и сила, и слава во веки. Аминь.

# SAMOAN

Mau
Mataio 6:9–13

6:9
O lea ia outou tatalo ai e tusa ma le ala lenei: Lo matou Tama
e o i le lagi, ia paia lou suafa.

6:10
O mai lou malo. Ia faia lou finagalo i le lalolagi, e pei ona faia
i le lagi.

6:11
Aumai ia i tatou i le aso nei a tatou meaai i aso taitasi.

6:12
Ma ia faamagalo mai ia i matou i a matou aitalafu, e pei ona
matou faamagaloina ai i latou o e aitalafu mai ia i matou.

6:13
Ma aua e te taitaiina i tatou i le faaosoosoga, ae laveai i tatou
mai le leaga: Aua o lou malo, ma le mana, ma le mamalu, e
faavavau. Amene.

# SEPEDI

Lengwalo
Mateo 6:9–13

**6:9**
Le rapela ka mokgwa wo: Tatago rena yo a lego magodimong, leina la gago a le kgethelwe.

**6:10**
Mmušo wa gago o tle. Thato ya gago e dirwe mo lefaseng, bjalo ka ge e dirwa legodimong.

**6:11**
Re fe lehono bogobe bja rena bja letšatši le letšatši.

**6:12**
Gomme o re swarele melato ya rena, bjalo ka ge re lebalela ba re kolotago.

**6:13**
O se re iše molekong, eupša o re hlakodiše bobeng, gobane mmušo le maatla le letago ke tša gago go iša mehleng ya neng le neng. Amene.

# SERBIAN

Свето писмо
Mattxew 6:9–13

6:9
После овог наиина моли се, Оие наљ који си на небесима, свети
се име твоје.

6:10
Да доре царство твоје. Нека буде воља твоја на земљи, као љто
је на небу.

6:11
Хлеб наљ насуљни дај нам данас.

6:12
И опрости нам наље дугове, као љто опраљтамо наљим
дућницима.

6:13
И не уведи нас у искуљење, него нас избави од зла, јер твоје је
краљевство, и мож, и слава, заувек. Амин.

# SESOTHO

Lengolo
Mattheu 6:9–13

6:9
Ka hona le rapele ka mokgwa ona: Ntata rona ya mahodimong,
lebitso la hao le ke le kgethehe!

6:10
'Muso oa hao o tle. Thato ea hao e etsoe lefatšeng, joalokaha
e etsahala leholimong.

6:11
U re fe kajeno bohobe ba r na ba letsatsi le letsatsi.

6:12
'Me u re tšoarele melato ea r na, joalokaha le r na re tšoarela
ba nang le melato ho r na.

6:13
O se ke wa re isa molekong, o mpe o re lopolle bobeng:
Hobane mmuso ke wa hao, le matla, le kganya, ka ho sa
feleng. Amen.

# SHONA

Rugwaro
Mateo 6:9–13

6:9
Naizvozvo imi nyengeterai sezvizvi: Baba vedu vari kudenga, zita renyu ngarikudzwe noutsvene.

6:10
Umambo hwenyu ngahuuye. Kuda kwenyu ngakuitwe panyika sezvakunoitwa kudenga.

6:11
Tipei nhasi chingwa chedu chamazuva namazuva.

6:12
Mutikanganwire mhosva dzedu, sezvatinokanganwira vane mhosva nesu.

6:13
Musatipinza pakuidzwa, asi mutisunungure pakuipa, nokuti ushe ndohwenyu, nesimba, nokubwinya nokusingaperi. Ameni, Ameni, Ameni.

# SINDHI

صحيفو
متٰي 6:9-13


**6:9**

نان آسمان ۾ ڪيجيٛءُ اج پا اسان :اسا پوءِدعا ڪريو: اسان اج پا ڪيجيٛءُوڪ آسمان ت
۾ ، تنهنجوان لولٻ ڪاپ ڇجي. تنهنڪريرنهن طريقي ڪان پوءِدعا ڪريو

**6:10**

تنهنجنهن آسمان ۾ آهي. چي باداشاهيٛ اچي. تنهنجنهن مرضي زمين ۾ پوري تئيٛ ، جهّزۡءَطرح
آسمان ۾ آهي.

**6:11**

نه هنهنٹنيڙي ڪي نان اسا ي مانيٛ ازانيٛ ڪي ڙيٛ ويڏ.

**6:12**

ءَ اسا ڪي نان اج قرض معاف ڪرڪ، جيئنَ اسان پهنهنجنرردضارن ڪي
معاف ڪريون.

**6:13**

ءَ اسا ڪي نان باداشاهيٛ ج ناهوتَ، شاش ءَ تاقات تي هميشہ لاءَ.آمين نَ
توهانَ ي باداشاهت، تاقات ءَ شان آهي، ۾ هميشہ لاءَ.آمين نَيٛ

86

# SINHALA

ශුද්ධ ලියවිල්ල
මතෙව් 6:9–13


6:9
මෙ ් ආකාරයෙන් පසුව, ඔබ යාච්ඤා කරන්න: ස්වර්ගයෙහි
වැඩ සිටින අපගෙ ් පියාණනේ, ඔබගේ නාමයට ගෞරව
වේවා.

6:10
ඔබගේ රාජ්‍යය පැමිණේවා. ඔබගේ කැමැත්ත
ස්වර්ගයෙහි මෙන් පොළොවෙහෝද සිදුවේවා.

6:11
අපගේ දෛනික ආහාරය අද අපට දෙන්න.

6:12
අපගේ ණයගැතියන්ට අප සමාව දෙන ලෙසම අපගේ
ණය අපට සමාව දෙන්න.

6:13
අපව පරීක්ෂාවට ගෙන නොයවා, නපුරෙන් අපව
ගලවාගත මැනව: මක්නිසාද රාජ්‍යය, බලය සහ මහිමය
සදහටම ඔබ සතුය. ආමෙන්.

# SLOVAK

Písmo
Matúš 6:9–13

6:9
Takto sa teda modlite: Ot e náš, ktorý si na nebesiach, posvä sa meno tvoje.

6:10
Prí krá ovstvo tvoje. Bu vô a tvoja ako v nebi, tak aj na zemi.

6:11
Chlieb náš každodenný daj nám dnes.

6:12
A odpus nám naše viny, ako aj my odpúš ame svojim vinníkom.

6:13
A neuve nás do pokušenia, ale zbav nás zlého, lebo tvoje je krá ovstvo i moc i sláva na veky. Amen.

# SLOVENIAN

Sveto pismo
Matej 6:9–13

**6:9**
Molite torej takole: O e naš, ki si v nebesih, posve eno bodi tvoje ime.

**6:10**
Pridi tvoje kraljestvo. Zgodi se tvoja volja tako na zemlji kot v nebesih.

**6:11**
Daj nam danes naš vsakdanji kruh.

**6:12**
In odpusti nam naše dolge, kakor tudi mi odpuš amo svojim dolžnikom.

**6:13**
In ne vpelji nas v skušnjavo, ampak reši nas hudega: kajti tvoje je kraljestvo in mo  in slava na veke. Amen.

# SOMALI

Qorniinka
Matayos 6:9–13

6:9
Sidaas daraaddeed sidatan u tukada, Aabbahayaga jannada ku jirow, magacaagu quduus ha ahaado.

6:10
Boqortooyadaadu ha timaado. Doonistaada dhulka ha lagu yeelo sida jannada loogu yeelo.

6:11
Maanta na sii kibisteena maalinlaha ah.

6:12
Oo naga cafi qaamahayaga sidaasaannu u cafinnay kuwa noo qaamaysan.

6:13
Jirrabaadda ha noo kaxayn, laakiinse sharka naga du, waayo, boqortooyada iyo xoogga iyo ammaanta adigaa leh weligaaba. Aamiin.

# SPANISH

Escritura
Mateo 6:9–13

6:9
Vosotros, pues, oraréis así: Padre nuestro que estás en los cielos, santificado sea tu nombre.

6:10
Venga tu reino. Hágase tu voluntad, como en el cielo, así también en la tierra.

6:11
El pan nuestro de cada día, dánoslo hoy.

6:12
Y perdónanos nuestras deudas, como también nosotros perdonamos a nuestros deudores.

6:13
Y no nos dejes caer en tentación, mas líbranos del mal: porque tuyo es el reino, y el poder, y la gloria, por todos los siglos. Amén.

# SUNDANESE

Kitab Suci
Mateus 6:9–13

6:9
Ku sabab kitu, neneda kieu: Rama kami nu aya di sawarga, asmana Anjeun disucikeun.

6:10
Datang Karajaan Anjeun. Pangersa Gusti laksana di bumi, sapertos di sawarga.

6:11
Pasihan abdi dinten ieu tuangeun sadinten.

6:12
Jeung hampura dosa-dosa urang, sakumaha urang ngahampura ka nu boga hutang.

6:13
Jeung ulah nungtun kami kana godaan, tapi nyalametkeun kami tina jahat: Pikeun Yours Karajaan, jeung kakawasaan, jeung kamulyaan, salawasna. Amin, Amin, Amin.

# SWAHILI

Maandiko
Mathayo 6:9–13

6:9
Kwa hiyo ninyi salini hivi: Baba yetu uliye mbinguni, Jina lako litukuzwe.

6:10
Ufalme wako uje. Mapenzi yako yafanyike duniani kama huko mbinguni.

6:11
Utupe leo mkate wetu wa kila siku.

6:12
Na utusamehe deni zetu, kama sisi tunavyowasamehe wadeni wetu.

6:13
Na usitutie majaribuni, bali utuokoe na yule mwovu; Amina.

# SWEDISH

Skriften
Matteus 6:9–13

6:9
På detta sätt ber ni därför: Fader vår, du som är i himlen, helgat vare ditt namn.

6:10
Kom ditt rike. Ske din vilja på jorden, som i himlen.

6:11
Ge oss i dag vårt dagliga bröd.

6:12
Och förlåt oss våra skulder, som vi förlåter våra skyldiga.

6:13
Och led oss inte in i frestelse, utan rädd oss från det onda: ty ditt är riket och makten och äran i evighet. Amen.

# TAJIK

Навиштаҳо
Матто 6:9–13

6:9
Пас аз ин чунин дуо гӯед: Эй Падари мо, ки дар осмон аст, исми Ту муқаддас бод.

6:10
Малакути Ту биёяд. Иродаи Ту дар замин, чунон ки дар осмон аст, ба амал ояд.

6:11
Имрӯз нони ҳаррӯзаи моро ба мо деҳ.

6:12
Ва қарзҳои моро бибахш, чунон ки мо қарздорони худро мебахшем.

6:13
Ва моро ба васваса наандоз, балки моро аз бадӣ раҳоӣ деҳ: зеро ки Малакут ва қувват ва ҷалол то абад аз они туст. Омин.

# TAMIL

வேதம்
மத்தேயு 6:9–13

6:9
இவ்வாறு ஐபெம்பண்ணுங்கள்:
பரலோகத்திலிருக்கிற எங்கள் பிதாவே, உமது
நாமம் பரிசுத்தமாயிருக்கும்.

6:10
உன் இராஜ்யம் வந்தது.உமது சித்தம் பரலோகத்தில்
நடப்பதுபோல, பூமியிலும் நடக்கும்.

6:11
இன்று எங்கள் அன்றாட உணவை எங்களுக்குக்
கொடுங்கள்.

6:12
எங்கள் கடனாளிகளை நாங்கள் மன்னிப்பது
போல, எங்கள் கடன்களையும் மன்னிப்பாயாக.

6:13
நீர் எங்களைச் சோதனைக்கு உள்ளாக்காமல்,
தீமையிலிருந்து எங்களை இரட்சிப்பாயாக; ராஜ்யமும்
வல்லமையும் மகிமையும் என்றென்றைக்கும்
உம்முடையது. ஆமென்.

# TATAR

Изге Язма
Маттай 6:9–13

6:9

Шуңа күрә дога кылыгыз: Күктәге Атабыз, сезнең исемегез изге ителсен.

6:10

Синең патшалыгың кил. Синең ихтыярың күктәге кебек җирдә дә үтәлсен.

6:11

Бу көнне безгә көндәлек икмәк бир.

6:12

Бурычларыбызны кичергән кебек, бурычларыбызны да кичер.

6:13

Us Вәсвәсәгә бирмә, бәлки безне явызлыктан коткар: Синең патшалыгың, көчең һәм даның мәңге синеке. Амин.

# TELUGU

గ్రంథం
మత్తయి 6:9–13


6:9
ఈ విధంగా ప్రార్థించండి: పరలోకంలో ఉన్న మా తండ్రీ,
నీ పేరు పవిత్రమైనది.


6:10
నీ రాజ్యం వచ్చు. నీ చిత్తము పరలోకంలో నెరవేరినట్లుగా
భూమియందును నెరవేరును.


6:11
ఈ రోజు మా రోజువారీ ఆహారాన్ని మాకు ప్రసాదించు.


6:12
మరియు మేము మా రుణగ్రస్తులను క్షమించినట్లే మా
అప్పులను క్షమించుము.


6:13
మరియు మమ్ములను ప్రలోభాలకు గురిచేయకుము,
దుష్టత్వము నుండి మమ్మును విడిపించుము:
రాజ్యము, శక్తి మరియు మహిమ ఎప్పటికీ నీవే. ఆమెన్.

# THAI

พระคัมภีร์
มัทธิว 6:9–13

6:9
ดังนั้นจงอธิษฐานดังนี้: พระบิดาของเราผู้ทรงสถิตในสวรรค์ ขอให้
พระนามของพระองค์เป็นที่สักการะ

6:10
อาณาจักรของพระองค์มา พระประสงค์ของพระองค์จะสำเร็จในโลกเหมือน
ในสวรรค์

6:11
โปรดประทานอาหารประจำวันแก่เราในวันนี้

6:12
และโปรดยกโทษให้พวกเราเหมือนยกโทษให้ลูกหนี้ของเรา

6:13
และอย่านำเราไปสู่การทดลอง แต่ขอทรงช่วยเราให้พ้นจากความชั่วร้าย
เพราะอาณาจักร อำนาจ และสง่าราศีเป็นของพระองค์เป็นนิตย์ สาธุ.

# TIGRINYA

ቅዱሳት መጻሕፍቲ
ማቴ 6:9–13


6:9
እምበኣርከስ ከምዚ ጌርኩም ጸልዩ፤ ኣታ ኣብ ሰማያት ዘለኹም ኣቦና፡ ስምካ
ይቐደስ፡፡

6:10
መንግስትኻ ንዓ፡፡ ፍቓድካ ከምቲ ኣብ ሰማይ ዝፍጸም ኣብ ምድሪ ይኹን፡፡

6:11
ሎሚ መዓልቲ ዕለታዊ እንጌራና ሃበና፡፡

6:12
ዕዳና ድማ ይቕረ በለልና፡ ከምቲ ንሕና ንዕዳና ይቕረ ንብል፡፡

6:13
መንግስትን ሓይልን ክብርን ንዘለኣለም ናትካ እያ እሞ፡ ካብ ክፉእ ኣናግፈና
እምበር፡ ናብ ፈተና ኣይተእትወና፡፡ ኣሜን፡፡

# TSONGA

Tsalwa ra Matsalwa
Matewu 6:9–13

6:9
Hikokwalaho khongelani hi mukhuva lowu: "Tata wa hina la
nge matilweni, vito ra wena a ri kwetsimisiwe."

6:10
Mfumo wa wena a wu te. Ku rhandza ka wena a ku endliwe
laha misaveni, ku fana ni le tilweni.

6:11
Hi nyike namuntlha xinkwa xa hina xa siku na siku.

6:12
Naswona hi rivalele milandzu ya hina, tani hi leswi na hina hi
rivalelaka lava hi va kolotaka.

6:13
U nga hi yisi emiringweni, kambe u hi kutsula eka leswo biha,
hikuva mfumo ni matimba ni ku vangama i swa wena hilaha
ku nga heriki. Amen.

# TURKISH

kutsal yazı
Matta 6:9–13

6:9
Bu ekilde dua edin: Göklerdeki Babamız, Adın kutsal kılınsın.

6:10
Senin krallı ın geliyor. Senin iste in gökte oldu u gibi yerde de yapılacak.

6:11
Bugün bize günlük ekme imizi ver.

6:12
Ve borçlularımızı ba ı ladı ımız gibi, borçlarımızı da ba ı la.

6:13
Ve bizi ayartmaya yöneltme, ama bizi kötülükten kurtar: Çünkü krallık, güç ve yücelik sonsuza dek senindir. Amin.

# TURKMEN

Mukaddes .azgy
Matta 6:9–13

6:9
onu üçin dileg edi : Gökdäki Atamyz, ady yz mukaddes
bolsun.

6:10
Paty alygy geler. Seni islegi , gökdäki ýaly ýer ýüzünde
amala a syn.

6:11
Bu gün bize gündelik çöregimizi beri .

6:12
Karz berijilerimizi bagy laý ymyz ýaly, bergilerimizi hem
bagy la .

6:13
Bizi synaga salma , bizi ýamanlykdan halas edi , çünki
Paty alyk, güýç we öhrat bakydyr. Amin.

# UKRAINIAN

Писання
Матвія 6:9–13

6:9
Отже, моліться так: Отче наш, що єси на небесах, нехай святиться ім'я Твоє.

6:10
Нехай прийде царство Твоє. Нехай буде воля Твоя на землі, як і на небі.

6:11
Хліб наш насущний дай нам сьогодні.

6:12
І прости нам борги наші, як і ми прощаємо винуватцям нашим.

6:13
І не введи нас у спокусу, але визволи нас від лукавого, бо Твоє є царство, і сила, і
слава навіки. Амінь.

# URDU

کا پاک مالک
متی 6:9-13

**6:9**

اس کے بعد تم اس طرح دعا کرو کہ اے ہمارے باپ جو آسمان میں ہے تیرا نام مقدس ہے۔

**6:10**

تیری بادشاہی آئے گی۔ تیری مرضی زمین میں پوری کی جائے، جیسی آسمان میں ہے۔

**6:11**

آج ہمیں ہماری روز مرہ کی روٹی دے دو۔

**6:12**

اور ہمارے قرض معاف فرما جس طرح ہم اپنے قرضدوروں کو معاف کرتے ہیں۔

**6:13**

اور ہمیں آزمائش میں نہ لا بلکہ ہمیں برائی سے نجات دے۔ کیونکہ بادشاہی اور قدرت اور جلال ہمیشہ کے لئے تیری ہی ہے۔ آمین۔

# UZBEK

Muqaddas Kitob
Matto 6:9–13

6:9
Shunday qilib, ibodat qilinglar: Osmondagi Otamiz! Sening isming ulug'lansin!

6:10
Sening shohliging kelsin. Sening irodang osmonda bo'lgani kabi yerda ham bajo bo'lsin.

6:11
Bu kun bizga kundalik nonimizni bering.

6:12
Va biz qarzdorlarimizni kechirganimizdek, bizning qarzlarimizni ham kechir.

6:13
Va bizni vasvasaga duchor qilma, balki yovuzlikdan xalos qil, chunki shohlik, kuch va ulug'vorlik abadiy senikidir. Omin.

# VIETNAMESE

thánh thư
Ma-thi-ơ 6:9–13

6:9
Vậy các ngươi hãy cầu nguyện theo cách này: Lạy Cha chúng tôi ở trên trời, Danh Cha ược thánh.

6:10
Vương quốc của bạn ến. Ý Cha ược nên ở ất như trời.

6:11
Xin cho chúng con hôm nay lương thực hằng ngày.

6:12
Xin tha nợ chúng con như chúng con cũng tha kẻ có nợ chúng con.

6:13
Xin chớ ể chúng con sa chước cám dỗ, nhưng cứu chúng con khỏi sự dữ: Vì nước, quyền, vinh hiển ều thuộc về Cha ời ời. Amen.

# XHOSA

UMATEYU 6:9–13

6:9
Thandazani ngoko nina nenjenje: Bawo wethu osemazulwini, malingcwaliswe igama lakho.

6:10
Mabufike ubukumkani bakho. Makwenzeke ukuthanda kwakho nasemhlabeni, njengokuba kusenziwa emazulwini.

6:11
Siphe namhla isonka sethu semihla ngemihla.

6:12
Usixolele amatyala ethu, njengokuba nathi sibaxolela abo banamatyala kuthi.

6:13
Ungasingenisi ekuhendweni, sihlangule ebubini; ngokuba ubukumkani bubobakho, namandla, nozuko, kuse emaphakadeni asemaphakadeni. Amen.

# YORUBA

Iwe mimo
Mátíù 6:9–13

6:9
Báyìí ni kí ẹ máa gbadura: Baba wa tí  bẹ ní ọrun, Ọ̀wọ̀ ni orúkọ rẹ.

6:10
Ìjọba rẹ dé. Ìfẹ́ tìrẹ ni kí a ṣe ní ayé, gẹ́gẹ́ bí ti ọrun.

6:11
Fun wa li onjẹ ojojumọ wa li oni.

6:12
Ki o si dari awọn gbese wa jì wa, gẹ́gẹ́ bi awa ti ndariji awọn onigbese wa.

6:13
Má si fà wa sinu idanwo, ṣugbọn gbà wa lọwọ ibi: nitori ijọba ni tirẹ, ati agbara, ati ogo, lailai. Amin.

# ZULU

UmBhalo
Mathewu 6:9–13

6:9
Ngakho-ke anokhuleka kanje: Baba wethu osezulwini, malingcweliswe igama lakho.

6:10
Umbuso wakho mawuze. mayenziwe intando yakho emhlabeni njengasezulwini.

6:11
Usiphe namuhla isinkwa sethu semihla ngemihla.

6:12
Usithethelele amacala ethu, njengokuba nathi sibathethelela abanamacala kithi.

6:13
Ungasingenisi ekulingweni, kodwa usikhulule kokubi, ngokuba umbuso ungowakho, namandla, nenkazimulo, kuze kube phakade. Amen.

Printed in the United States
by Baker & Taylor Publisher Services